T0197322

A Guide for
Traumatized
Children

Joi Crawford-Johnson, Ph.D., M.A., CCC

WESTBOW
P R E S S®
A DIVISION OF THOMAS NELSON
& ZONDERVAN

WestBow Press books may be ordered through booksellers or by contacting:

WestBow Press
A Division of Thomas Nelson & Zondervan
1663 Liberty Drive
Bloomington, IN 47403
www.westbowpress.com
844-714-3454

The counseling sessions of the enclosed case study is by permission; and is based on counsel-ing sessions of four children whose names are unknown and protected.

Scripture taken from the King James Version of the Bible.

ISBN: 978-1-6642-2523-7 (sc)
ISBN: 978-1-6642-2524-4 (hc)
ISBN: 978-1-6642-2522-0 (e)

Library of Congress Control Number: 2021903771

Print information available on the last page.

WestBow Press rev. date: 03/22/2021

Counseling has a process that involves connecting with the counselee and keeping a good rapport with them. Generally, it takes time to connect with a client; especially if they have been traumatized. Initially connecting with a child who has been traumatized can be most difficult when they have been emotionally distressed by their predator. With the counselor displaying genuine compassion towards the child and having an amiable attitude with the child client can lead the child to feel free to speak. Making them feel comfortable enough to express their self is crucial in the counseling process and in overcoming what they are being counseled for.

The purpose of the counselee's session is to explore issues, help them with a plan, guiding them in their progression and eventually terminating the counseling session when you have spiritually discerned the counselee is strong enough to walk alone (without the counselor).

Children are a gift from God. They are vulnerable and easy to take advantage of because they believe easily. They have faith in what they hear. I believe; therefore, the God of the Bible tells us to have childlike faith. Jesus Christ uses children as an example for us. In *Matthew 18: 3-6*, Jesus was among the little children. He beckoned His disciples to be humble like children by saying, *Except ye be converted, and become as little children, ye shall not enter into the kingdom of heaven. Whosoever therefore shall humble himself as this little child, the same is greatest in the kingdom of heaven. And whoso shall receive one such little child in my name receiveth me. But whoso shall offend one of these little ones which believe in me, it were better for him that a millstone were hanged about his neck, and that he were drowned in the depth of the sea*[1].

For children to be healthy and whole, they need to be taught to love Jesus Christ and guided in the Scriptures. They should be around people who will guide them in the truth of God's Word with their best interests at heart. Some examples of these are parents, guardians, caregivers, teachers, and preachers.

---

[1] King James Version Bible. (2012). Holman King James Version Study Bible. Holman Bible Publishers Nashville, Tennessee

Today, children continue to be recognized as the future leaders of this world. Yet, at the same time, they are targeted like a bullseye for Satan's snare to snatch their future away from them through predators and all types of perversion. *First Peter 5:8* says, *Be sober, be vigilant; because your adversary the devil, as a roaring lion, walketh about, seeking whom he may devour:* We are commanded to *train up a child in the way he should go: and when he is old, he will not depart from it (Proverbs 22:6).* Children have purpose and a plan for their lives since before they were born. *Jeremiah 1:5 says, Before I formed thee in the belly I knew thee; and before thou camest forth out of the womb I sanctified thee, and I ordained thee a prophet unto the nations.* Their future is bright; and this is reflected in *Jeremiah 29:11, For I know the thoughts that I think toward you, saith the Lord, thoughts of peace, and not of evil, to give you an expected end[2].* We must protect our children and provide a haven to feed them spiritual food to fulfill God's plan for them.

Emotional and physical trauma in children occurs when a child is harmed and violated from an experience or a series of events that caused their behavior to be altered in a negative way

---

[2] King James Version Bible. (2012). Holman King James Version Study Bible. Holman Bible Publishers Nashville, Tennessee

that affects their daily lives and keeps them from their ability to interact with others. There are several traumatic events that can happen in the lives of children that without counseling can affect them socially as they grow older; and they are as follows: sexual abuse; physical abuse; bullying; domestic violence; the death of a loved one—to name a few. The effects of childhood trauma can cause a child to react to people and situations with a feeling of anxiety. Children who have experienced traumatic events will respond to an extreme if their psychological and physical well-being is threatened by the situation. Children who have been traumatized can be helped by a mental health counselor/specialist who is well established in the field of mental health abuse/psychological traumas and Christian counseling. They should first be screened, evaluated, or assessed to develop a trauma history. It is imperative that children who were traumatized receive counseling while they are young, or the effects of the trauma will affect their relationships as an adult. Overall, children need to be reassured that the traumatic event they went through is not their fault. The parents need to be able to patiently help guide the child back to a place or normalcy or to a place where the child can feel psychologically and physically safe and secure. The child needs to know or be reminded that they are loved, accepted, and appreciated.

Post-Traumatic Stress Disorder (PTSD) can be common among children who have experienced traumatic events. PTSD is a mental disorder that is triggered by a past traumatic event, in this case, in the child's life. However, if the parent recognizes this, they should have the child see a counselor. Asking the pediatrician or counselor questions will allow the child to receive the type of referral they need. Treatment for childhood trauma is not only having the child see a counselor. It's providing the right support, healthy relationships, not returning them to the person they were traumatized by or place where they were traumatized, creating a normalcy for the child—that is, giving them back a routine; being constructive and productive with them; complimenting them and encouraging good behavior—to name a few.

The Impact of Child Trauma/Abuse in America

The number of children experiencing trauma and abuse in the United States of America continues to grow faster than the abused child can get help. Child abuse and trauma is an experience that is nothing like a scar that can be bandaged, and antibiotic placed on it to heal in a few days. Childhood trauma is a horrifying experience with effects that can last a lifetime. Unfortunately, there are various types of child abuse and they are: child neglect, physical abuse, and sexual abuse—to name a few. With each, the child or children suffer.

Statistics shows the overall problem of child abuse. The

number of children abused allows the authorities to create and implement an intervention and a preventative measure that will protect them.

Although, there are several cases that are not reported, according to the National Children's Alliance[3], there is an estimated 678,000 children (unique incidents) who were victims of abuse and neglect in 2018, the most recent year for which there is national data. That is about 1% of kids each year.

Social workers and child protective services complete pursue investigations and avenues to protect more than 3.5 million children. Intervention is immediate and crucial for the child's safety as well as measures to prevent child abuse. An estimated 1.9 million children received prevention services.

When a child speaks and raises their voice about abuse and what they are experiencing as a result of it; it is helpful for them in order for their perpetrator to be accosted and placed under arrest to stop taking advantage of children who are considered vulnerable.

Child abuse is a deadly act if the predator is not caught in time. According to the National Children's Alliance, in 2018,

---

[3] https://www.nationalchildrensalliance.org/media-room/national-statistics-on-child-abuse/

an estimated 1,770 children died from abuse and neglect in the United States.

Just last year, in 2020, I remember a case of a man who sexually abused his infant daughter; and eventually she died because she bled profusely. Her diaper was filled with blood. In my opinion, her dad was extremely sick minded with more than mental health issues.

Unfortunately, out of each of the three types of child abuse— child neglect, sexual abuse and physical abuse--, child neglect is the most common. The National Children's Alliance reported that three-out-of-five (nearly 61%) of victims were neglected only, more than 10% were physically abused only, and 7% were sexually abused only. Yet the statistics indicate a more complex problem where children experience multiple forms of abuse. In 2018, more than 15% of kids were polyvictimized (suffered two or more forms of abuse) (National Children's Alliance).

Other organizations have investigated child abuse cases and have alleged that there are many disclosed cases that have not been fully completed. Therefore, the results of the child abuse case (especially child sexual abuse cases) are not indicated; and those cases include charges and convictions.

One of the ways to end child sexual abuse, child neglect and physical child abuse is by listening a child who is a victim of child abuse, immediately report any wrong doing against a child that portrays any type of abuse. Although it may be difficult to report an abusive parent (who is more than likely the predator), it is crucial for the child's well-being. On the other hand, since the child loves their parent or the person who is close to them who is an abuser, the child can feel rejected and become angry because their parent was taken away or they were taken away from their loved one. There are hotline telephone numbers for people to call; as well as calling 9-1-1. Since children are valuable, they should always be the priority.

Child Trauma and Extensive Counseling

SESSION 1

Sammy's Negative Thinking

I began counseling a child who has contemplated suicide. Below are simulations of the sessions that we have been having to help him understand, cope with, and overcome the thoughts of suicide and deep chronic depression. It was a long process to get whom I will call "Sammy," to realize there is a war going on in our mind and we, with our spirit, have to bring our thoughts under the subjection of the Holy Spirit. This had to be convincing on a child's level because "Sammy," whose name is fictitious, is a child.

I met with "Sammy." "Sammy" is a young boy. Since this was the first-time meeting with him, we met at a location that he was familiar with and felt comfortable at. Come to find out, where we met was one of his favorite places to visit.

Before the session began, the father of "Sammy" completed and sign a parental consent form which gave me permission to counsel "Sammy" since he is a minor. In addition, his father completed a personal history form on behalf of Sammy to give me more information about him for the next session. For cases such as Sammy's it is recommended that he has more than one session. For a suicide attempt, there should be as many sessions as possible depending on how the client responds to the previous session.

Sammy arrived with his other siblings. When I greeted Sammy and his siblings, I gave each one a small candy bag with a toy. Sammy's had the biggest toy since he was my client at the time. His brother was glad to receive his candy bag but was looking for a big toy as well.

We walked over to where the counseling session was going to be held. The location was at a bright and colorful room where other children and their families met to eat and socialize. Although there were babies there as well, they did not distract

Sammy or me from the session. While at the table, diagonally away from us was his siblings. I began the counseling session with prayer. After asking Sammy if he knew why he was there, he said he did not know. His dad said he told him the night before. His dad also gave me permission to remind him about suicide.

Sammy's body language showed he was nervous because he kept rocking side to side. He also blinked a lot. I presented Sammy with questions that will let me know where he was at psychologically and emotionally at the time. However, when I asked him questions about his mother, he did not react. Sammy was frozen with a serious expression on his face. He looked as if he was thinking hard; as well as looked puzzled. This was when I asked him how he felt about his mom.

Before counseling Sammy, I gave his parent literature about suicide; what the Bible says about suicide; daily affirmations for children; the role of the child; the role of parents; and how a child can begin their process now to achieving their goal. The following is a copy of the questions asked to Sammy from the "Intake Form for Children" which I created to assist me in counseling him and to be used for any initial counseling session with children. The child must be informed in advance that there will be questions asked that may bring up uncomfortable feelings. Reassure the child that it is okay, and they can discuss those feelings:

What is your name?

How old are you?

How are you feeling right now?

Do you know why we are meeting?

How's school?

Do you like school?

How do you feel about your teacher?

How do you feel about your classmates?

What is your favorite subject? Why?

Do you have friends/best friend in school?

Do you have a best friend where you live?

Are there bullies in your school?

What punishment do the children get in school if they misbehave or do something against the rules?

Have you ever been punished in school? Why? What was it?

Have you ever been punished at home? Why? What was it?

What is your favorite sport?

What is your favorite TV show?

Do you like to watch movies?

What is your favorite movie?

What is your favorite place to visit?

What is your favorite part of the day (morning, noon, night)? Why?

Are you afraid of anything? What? Why?

Is there a saddest time in your life that you remember?

What is the happiest time in your life you can remember?

Are you happy right now?

What makes you happy?

What makes you sad?

Do you feel you are treated fairly?

How do you feel about your siblings?

Are you happy at home? (If not, why?)

Are you scared at home? (If so, why?)

How do you feel about dad?

What is your idea of a father? Or how do you think fathers should treat you?

How does he show you love?

How do you feel about mom?

How does she show you love?

What is your idea of a mother? Or how do you think a mother should treat you?

How does mom and dad show love to each other?

How do you feel about yourself? Do you think you are a good child? (Affirm them)

What do you want to be when you grow up? (Encourage the child on how to achieve goal; and they can be the best "whatever it is they're want to be").

After asking these questions, I spoke with Sammy briefly about the critical answers that he gave regarding self-harm. He expressed more than once that his siblings tease him and call him names. It seems he was almost overcome by the constant name calling along with his living situation—having to visit his mother while living with his father.

It was about time to end the session because the attention span for a child is not so long and you want to keep their attention for them to answer the questions. I ended the session by reiterating and reinforcing his right to stand against name calling and to tell his father if it continues so his father can do something about it. Sammy's parent and I scheduled the next session for him; and it was the next week; but in a different location.

SESSION 2
Affirming Sammy & Promoting Positive Thinking

Session two was in the morning at a library in the children's section. When I gave Sammy a notebook/journal as a gift to write his feelings, he smiled. I asked him about his weekend. He said it was good; but was upset because his sister kept playing the "moo" song and did not stop. He said he told his mom, but she did not listen—she brushed him off. His dad asked him if he feels powerless when he is brushed off? Sammy said yes. Sammy's dad said he will speak with Sammy's sister and mother regarding this. After Sammy shared his feelings, I focused on Sammy's identity—giving him an understanding of who he is so he can focus on himself and not what others (such as his sister) are doing while he has to be present in their surroundings.

Another issue that Sammy contended with was that it is dark when he sleeps on the floor at night in the living room. Sammy's dad said he will send night lights.

Sammy's dad contacted me to let me know that Sammy lied about feeling powerless when he said he told his mother he feels powerless when he tells his mother. He said he never told his mother about his sister playing the song. Sammy's dad apologized and realized his wrong. I did wonder as we proceed with more sessions if Sammy would lie again; and if he does, how can I be of help to him. I continued with the next session without negatively labeling Sammy.

SESSION 3
Sammy & His Siblings: How They Felt About Each Other

This session was to implement the importance of knowing who they are and the dangers of name-calling. I was prepared to ask Sammy's siblings the following questions:

How can we keep a good relationship with each other?

What can cause a bad relationship?

Sammy expressed how bad he felt when he is called names by his siblings.

The counseling session expanded to an on-the-spot assignment with Sammy and his siblings writing a description of their self in three words; describe their siblings in three words; write three things they liked about each other and three things they disliked about each other. They seemed to be excited about this assignment because they knew they were not going to be reprimanded for expressing their feelings.

The results of the findings of the descriptions by Sammy and his siblings were as followed:

Sammy described himself as sensitive, smart, and kind. He was described by his siblings as: a tattler, nice sometimes, stubborn, smart, silly brave, mean and mostly nice. Things they liked/disliked about Sammy was that he plays with them; he's nice sometimes and acts like a big brother; he tattles too much; he calls names, acts like a bully and hits people.

Sibling #1 was described their self as very mean, only mentally pretty to God, mean. Sibling #1's siblings described them as: kind most of the time, smart, brave, hard worker, unkind, annoying, and mean. Things that were liked and disliked by Sibling #1's siblings were as followed: kind, has courage, most of the time is nice and not really mean, plays with me; calls me names, says I have a big head shaped like a square, big old tattle-tale, mean, disrespectful, annoying.

Sibling #2 described their self as silly and smart. Sibling #2's siblings described them as: smart, brave, silly, annoying, and unkind. The likes and dislikes about Sibling #2 are as follows:

kind, courage, plays with me, silly and not mean; calls names, mean.

Sibling #3 described their self as smart, silly. Sibling #3's siblings described them as nice sometimes, kind, courage, really funny and nice; annoying, interrupts too much, yells and talks over people, denies things, steals things, doesn't get in trouble, and a big old tattle-tale.

Since name-calling was the common issue among Sammy and his siblings, I emphasized who they are to them and the importance of addressing each other by their name or the positive they represent. We did role play with one calling the other a positive name. As a result, the sibling who was called a name smiled; and when called a negative name they frowned. Placing emphasis on positive names gives strength, power and speaks life to one another. In addition to explaining to the siblings about name-calling, I presented Scriptures from the Holy Bible about name-calling. The Scriptures are as follows:

Proverbs 12:18

Ecclesiastes 10:12-14

Matthew 5:22

Luke 6:31

John 8:43-44

Colossians 3:7-8

Ephesians 4:29-31 [4].

This session was crucial for Sammy because name-calling was one of the reasons why he attempted suicide. The father was concerned about sibling #1 of their description of their self as "very mean" and asked me to discuss that at the next session.

SESSION 4
Sammy & His Siblings

We met at a church for this session. Sammy and his siblings seemed sleepy yet playful. That morning, they had just come from visiting their mother and seemed a bit hyperactive. They said they enjoyed their stay. After the children arrived, they were very talkative and playful. They greeted me with hugs. They seemed very lively and bubbly. I asked them how their weekend was with their mother and they said it was good. During their visit, they played video games, watched YouTube and television. They, especially Sibling #2, expressed how Sammy did not have

---

[4] King James Version Bible. (2012). Holman King James Version Study Bible. Holman Bible Publishers Nashville, Tennessee

a good time while visiting his mother because he was mad the whole time. Sammy seemed a bit sluggish this morning during the session. He is not happy going to his mother's place but wants to see her. Sibling #3 was smiling as usual and express the good time during her visitation. Sibling #1 was very talkative, smiling and answering questions for everyone about their visit.

I handed them their completed form about how they felt about each other (likes/dislikes). They began to draw and doodle on the back of the form. Each child drew something creative and interesting while I was talking with them. Sibling #3 drew boy and girl superheroes on the back of his form. The superheroes are fighting each other in pairs. One superhero has energy or electricity coming from it as it captures its enemy who looks to be like another superhero. The other superhero looks to have captured her enemy with flames of fire in which he is about to fall on.

Sibling #1 brought up a feeling that was never discussed. Sibling #1 said they feel they are the blame for their father and mother not married and living together and they do not like going to two homes. Sibling #1 is 12 years old and remembers the time when there was no visitation, and they were one happy family.

This is what Sibling #1 meant when they described their self as "very mean." They were feeling hurt and not mean. They are hurt that they are going through a family crisis which includes divorce and a drastic change from what they were used to. I expressed to Sibling #1 that the situation between their mother and father is by no means their fault—that they love Sibling #1 and what happened to their parents is the decision of the parents not having to do with Sibling #1. Sibling #1 listened; but still felt that way. The father was saddened by just learning how his child felt. He thought it would be best if I met with Sibling #1 separately so she could have the opportunity to express her feelings without distraction. Her siblings were busy doing their own thing during this session.

SESSION 5
Individual Counseling With Sibling #1

The scheduling of the sessions began to change for Sammy and his siblings. We began to meet virtually. The winter season also included influenza season and other sickness and diseases which changed everyone's schedule and impacted them socially, economically, emotionally—to name a few. In addition to what people have already been suffering with, they have developed depression and anxiety to a more heightened degree. Depression and anxiety know no age, race, creed, and ethnicity. It seems to wait for things to go wrong for a person to allow it to enter in.

Because Sammy had attempted suicide weeks ago, it was a concern of mine regarding how he was handling his thoughts since we were not able to meet in person. During this session, Sammy had improved since our first session. He said he no longer had thoughts of harming himself. Each sibling had their turn for a counseling session which was thirty minutes each.

It was Sibling #1's turn for a counseling session. During the last session, she dropped a "bombshell" when she revealed that she feels "it's her fault that her mom and dad are divorced." The reason why she said she feels "mean" is because she does not want to visit her mother while living with her father. She wants to remain in one place like it was when she grew up with both parents (who are divorced).

In my research to prepare to counsel Sibling #1, I searched the dictionary for a simple definition to give her; along with the Holy Bible to find Scriptures related to being "mean" and "hurt" to give her an understanding of what she was feeling. In addition,

I explained to her what hurt can lead to—bitterness, sickness, anxiety, depression—to name a few. With Sibling #1 feeling this way while knowing it wasn't her fault that she felt this way, I was determined to give her words of comfort as I wished I could change her thinking to understand that when parents disagree, it's not the child's fault. I asked Sibling #1 if her mother knows that she is hurting. She said, no. I asked her if she talks to her mother and she said, "not often, and she doesn't listen most of the time." She expressed that her mother feels that what she does is her choice. She was satisfied discussing it with her dad; and she does feel comfortable talking to her mom.

After presenting this information to Sibling #1, she realized that she was "hurt" and not "mean" in regards to how she was feeling because things were not the way it used to be when she used to live with both parents without having visitation rights with her mother. The Scriptures were as follows:

Psalms 34:18

Mark 11:25

1 Corinthians 13:1-13

2 Peter 3:9

1 John 1:9

Romans 9:19

Titus 1:2[5].

Sibling #1 was reminded of what can cause hurt feelings and its triggers. We discussed the alternative to hurt feelings and what she can do when she begins to feel hurt again. Sibling #1 was informed that we can change things that we go through, but we can change how we handle situations. I implemented treatment for Sibling #1 and ways in which she can deal with her hurt feelings; and encouraged her to continue to be a good daughter to her parents, as well as a good sister to her siblings. I gave Sibling #1 a notebook to use to journal her feelings whether she feels hurt or happy.

SESSION 6
Virtual Counseling With Sammy & His Siblings

The goal in this session was to affirm Sammy and his siblings through biblical stories—something they can relate to. However, it was necessary to first re-cap the last session with Sibling #1.

---

[5] King James Version Bible. (2012). Holman King James Version Study Bible. Holman Bible Publishers Nashville, Tennessee

It was about ten o'clock in the morning when Sibling #1 and I met. From my observation, she appeared to comfortable and relaxed with her bedtime clothes on and her hair wrapped. She was very attentive sitting on the bottom of her bunk bed. There were a few questions that I asked Sibling #1 to let her know that she matters to me:

How are you and did you sleep well? She said she had a good sleep.

What have you been doing since we last met? Did you write in your new notebook? She said, yes and that she writes down her thoughts and her feelings and stuff. I told her that good because it makes a difference in expressing her feelings and in getting them out.

What have your siblings been doing lately? She said they have not been fighting.

I let Sibling #1 know that I will be asking some questions that may bring up some uncomfortable feelings and that if it does, it's okay and we will talk about those feelings and that's a good way for it to come out. Thereafter, I shared with Sibling #1 that I've been concerned about her regarding our last session because she mentioned she felt it was her fault that her parents are not together because they argue and mention names; she doesn't enjoy going to two places to see her mom and dad; that she felt hurt; and that she had a dream about living with both parents. She feels like she cannot wait until she is 18 years of age so she can do what she wants to do. I reiterated and emphasized that she is loved by both parents no matter what happened, it's not her fault because of whatever decision they make; and I understand her wanting to be 18 years old so she can get the space that she desires to not feel involved with her parents' tough challenges. I let her know that being 18 years old somewhat gives you an opportunity to be on your own; and, at the same time, 18 years old means being more responsible.

I asked Sibling #1 what she does when those hurt feelings arise. She began thinking. She mentioned that she writes in her notebook since our last session. I reminded her that she said she had hurt feelings because of her visitation rights with her mother. She said she still feels it is her fault that things are the way they are. I encouraged Sibling #1 by letting her know that what she's going through is no surprise to God; and that He knew she was going to experience this; that He loves her and wants her to go through this with Him—that is, include Jesus in what she's going through by talking to Him about it. I made her aware that there are situations that we cannot change; but we can change what we do and how we handle what we go through just as the *Hebrew three boys while in the fiery furnace according to the Book of Daniel*[6].

Sibling #1 remembered the Bible story of the Hebrew three boys in the fiery furnace when compared to what she is going through. I told her she has no control over the situation. She and her siblings "fell down" bound in their situation (fiery furnace); that she must remember that Jesus is with her while she is going through having visitation rights. I let her know that she does not have to accept the hurt that tries to grip her. *Daniel 3:25* says they have no hurt while walking in the fiery furnace. God will promote her and her siblings after going through just as King Nebuchadnezzar promoted the three Hebrew boys *(Daniel 3:30)*[7].

To help alleviate the hurt that Sibling #1 feels while going through, it was important for her to remember her role as a daughter to her parents and in doing this she is pleasing God

---

[6] King James Version Bible. (2012). Holman King James Version Study Bible. Holman Bible Publishers Nashville, Tennessee

[7] King James Version Bible. (2012). Holman King James Version Study Bible. Holman Bible Publishers Nashville, Tennessee

because He said to honor her father and her mother; and that God will bring her out in His time. I encouraged her to talk to God, talk to her dad, talk to her mother and she can even call me as a confidant.

As the session was at a close, I gave her an assignment that consists of three things until the next time we meet:

1. Take 5 minutes talking to God.

2. 10 minutes to read Psalm 139:14 and write what it means to her.

3. 15 minutes doing something constructive that she enjoys (ex: manicure, drawing).

SESSION 7
Virtual Counseling With Sammy

It was Sammy's turn to be counseled. After asking Sammy about how he is doing and how homeschooling is going. He expressed that he missed his friends; but he still talks to them. He said he feels bad about sickness and diseases existing in the world. He said he wake up early in the morning for a class meeting. (While speaking with Sammy, just as a child does, he made "bugs bunny" faces as he could see himself in the laptop; and began sticking his tongue out which was very funny to me.) He expressed that he wants to go back to school.

We spoke about his last visit to his mother's place. He said his siblings did not call him names except once or twice; everything was normal; he did not feel sad; and his siblings stopped talking mean to him. One of the major victories is that Sammy said he did not contemplate harming himself and that journaling helps him feel better. He expressed that he talks to God at mostly at night. He said that he is still writing in his notebook. He likes to write a prayer, draw, and write his feelings. When he visited his mother's home,

I encourage Sammy to practice what his dad is teaching and training him; and as he does this, he will become stronger than what made him mad. In addition, I reminded him that he has a mission—a role as a child to his parents to honor them and as he does that he is, at the same time, honoring God. I gave Sammy an assignment for the next session:

Continue talking to God.

10 minutes to read and study what *Judges 6:12* means to him—*"And the angel of the Lord appeared unto him (Gideon), and said unto him, The Lord is with thee, thou mighty man of valor"* (courage,

strength)[8]. I also gave him to read, study and write what *1John 4:4* means to him.

15 minutes doing something constructive just for himself (ex: drawing, games, toys).

The take-away that I gave Sammy was to remember that Jesus is with him during his visitation with his mother.

SESSION 8
Virtual Counseling With Sammy & His Siblings

I met with Sammy first. He said he woke up early for a class meeting. He was making faces in the camera on the device he was using for his counseling session.

We did a recap of the last session. He expressed that he feels bad about diseases because he said it is worse than the flu. He expressed how much he wanted to return to the school building.

I reminded him that as he practices what his dad is teaching him, he will become stronger than what makes him mad or angry.

---

[8] King James Version Bible. (2012). Holman King James Version Study Bible. Holman Bible Publishers Nashville, Tennessee

Sibling #3 was next in line to meet. He was hidden so that I can only see his eyebrows and up. He said he was feeling good. He had already had his exercise, prayed, and completed his schoolwork. His personality is a lot different from Sammy's. Sibling #3 said he kind of likes being home from school although he misses his friends. He said he has been praying about that. He desires to at least see his friends on the computer during school session. (Sibling #3 is busy during the sessions. He continued going in and out of the camera.) His feelings changed since the last time we met. After asking him about the name-calling by his siblings—sibling #4 said there has not been much name-calling.

It was Sibling #4's turn to be counseled. I asked her how she enjoys staying home—learning virtually. She said she likes staying home because she does not like school anyway. Her favorite time in school is recess. She said reading and spelling makes her have a headache and she does not like math and science. In school she used to do exercises like stretching and yoga, but she does not like it because it's boring, she says.

I asked Sibling #4 about her mom. She said her mom works on the weekends; so, she picks her and her siblings up after work on weekends or dad picks them up.

Sibling #4 said there was no name-calling that she made against her siblings and no one called her bad names. She said no one has been mean to her and she hasn't been *mean* to anyone.

Sibling #4 had much to discuss about what she enjoyed. She said that her sister, Sibling #1, ordered about 115 dolls on her phone. She began naming the dolls: *Ravee, Roxanna, Hazel, Harmony (who has raggedy hair), Carrington, Jessica, and Annabel.* She said they are *Barbie's* babies. *Daniella* is too.

She did not miss going to mom's place she said. When she goes to mom's place, she stays three days; and stays at dad's place for 5 days. She said sometimes she feels like going to mom's place, but she is not allowed to bring her dolls. Whatever is at mom's place, stays at mom's place and whatever is at dad's place, stays at dad's place.

Going over to her grandmother's house is fun because she gets to bring toys home. One of reasons why she likes going to her mom's place is because she gets to go to her grandmother's house because there is candy there; and her grandmother gives her gifts. She said her sibling (Sibling #1) has more dolls because of the gifts.

Sibling #4 had many conversations—talking about whatever came to her mind. She mentioned that the store, Game Stop, is going out of business; that her eldest sibling does many things with her dolls; for example: when someone shook the doll, the doll's eye came out. Lastly, Sibling #4 mentioned that she prefers going to her grandmother's house because she lets her, and her siblings do what they want.

Sibling #1 was the last to be counseled. Her mood was nonchalant. She didn't seem as if she was interested in having a counseling session although it was important to her dad for her to have this type of platform to be able to share her thoughts and at the same time, receive wise counsel. She said she wanted to go to her mom's house but was kind of ok with not going. She does not enjoy talking much but would rather be quiet.

I questioned her about her and the relationship of her siblings. She said that Sibling #3 called Sammy a bad name. I asked her how he reacted, and she said he told Sibling #3 to stop and he kicked him. I asked if anyone told their dad and she said no; and that dad did not know yet, so she tried to stop them.

After asking Sibling #1 if she was still writing in her journal, she said she has been writing in it; she said she talks to God on her own and she and her family (siblings and dad) pray together every day.

She mentioned that mom works on the weekend; and they see her on half days on Fridays although she would like to see her like a normal weekend. While Sibling #1 was speaking she seemed a little sad as she expressed that she wants to go to one place to see her mom and that is also at her dad's house. She said she realizes it a little bit that she is not the cause of her parents being separated. I asked her what makes her realize it is not her fault and she said that her mom told her, but she still does not know what she feels.

SESSION 9
Personality Type Of Sammy And His Siblings

Sammy was the first one to be counseled to discuss his personality type, traits and needs. The goal for this session was to discuss how Sammy and I can use his positive and negative traits when interacting with his siblings and others. I explained to him what the definition of personality is—the combination of characteristics or qualities that form an individual's distinctive character. For example: a sunny personality is a personality that is very engaging.

I told Sammy that his personality type is color-coded and the traits for the color he portrayed was orange. Orange stands for a type of person who is adventurous and who enjoys social communication. The aspects of Orange personality are as follows:

Effects of orange: enthusiasm; rejuvenation; courage; vitality

Positive traits: sociable, optimistic, enthusiastic, cheerful, self-confident, independent, flamboyant, extroverted, and uninhibited, adventurous, the risk-taker, creative flair, warm-hearted, agreeable, and informal

Negative traits: superficial and insincere, dependent, over-bearing, self-indulgent, the exhibitionist, pessimistic, inexpensive, unsociable, and overly proud

If favorite color: You move on easily from life's setbacks; having patience can be very difficult; you can be forceful and domineering at times which can happen when you're stressed and overwhelmed; you're indecisive, inconsistent and unpredictable; you may be an unkind practical joker; when you feel fearful it is shown though feeling knots in your stomach

Deepest need: is to be with people to socialize with them and be accepted and respected as part of a group

If orange is your dislike color: you are not comfortable in large groups; you do not like partying and socializing; you are more comfortable with a small circle of friends; you don't like flamboyance and showing off; you may be holding yourself back socially; and anger can indicate that you have been mistreated cruelly at some stage in your life.

It was important for Sammy to know that he was not negatively labeled by the negative traits especially because of the reason he initially came for counseling. What I emphasized to Sammy was his identity in Christ. Since Sammy is claiming salvation, he was able to receive and be reminded of who God says he is.

I discussed with Sammy how he can use his traits and needs. Since he's fun-loving, outgoing and a risk-taker, I encouraged him to add fun to his chores such as pretending his clothes is a basketball and to shoot it in the hamper or washing machine; to sing and dance while he's picking up things off the floor and putting them away. In addition to this fun, pretending he is a construction worker at a junk yard while straightening up; racing to fold clothes or putting them away makes cleaning up fun too.

Since Sammy and Sibling 4 have a challenging relationship in a negative way, I found it interesting, yet, not surprising that they are similar in personality. Sibling 4 is quiet, fun, outgoing, and sociable just like Sammy. Sammy expressed that she bothers him and is mean to him through name-calling.

I asked Sibling 4 if she knows what the word personality means, and she said she heard of the word. After informing her about what the word means and giving examples, I emphasized her identity [in Christ] and encouraged her to use the traits of "Orange personality" to treat her brother better where they "bump heads;" as well as gave her an understanding of why she does the things she does in general.

Since Sammy came to me for counseling initially because of his suicide attempt, my greatest concern was not only that Sammy would harm himself; but he could possibly harm his siblings (especially Sibling #4).

In the counseling session with Sibling #4, I shared with her that because her personality involves boredom, feeling lazy, that she loves people as well as to talk and communicate with others; she is going to have to know when to be quiet and that there's a time for everything. When it comes to her relating with Sammy, she should wait until he invites her to play with him—that she cannot demand his attention because it's not a good thing to do and that can harm her relationship with him instead of improve it. I reminded her that she and her siblings have a father and a mother to give them instructions. Therefore, there is no need for her to tell Sammy or her other siblings what to do in a demanding way. I encouraged her to continue to speak using good words, go to her dad if there's a problem, and to leave it up to him to make a decision on what should go on in their household. Sibling #4's response was that they're mean to her, hit her and call her names—especially Sammy.

After meeting with them individually, I met with Sammy and Sibling #4 to see if I can be the mediator to help them get along better. While they were sitting together, Sammy was upside down and Sibling #4 was giggling a lot. I encouraged them to find something to do together that they can equally enjoy. I reminded them that they are both leaders. However, they must lead their self into doing what they are supposed to do; and not to make their good quality into something bad (challenging in a negative way). I encouraged them to be good leaders, respectful to each other and to keep their hands to their self; and that I will check in upcoming sessions if they are doing this.

Sibling #3 was next for a counseling session to discuss his personality type which is "Yellow Personality." His father said that this personality test was "most accurate" out of each personality test for each child. Children with "Yellow Personality" are people pleasers; they avoid conflicts; they are kind; they are concerned about other people's opinion; they can be very indecisive; they tend to depend on people heavily to make decisions so that they don't disappoint anyone; they tend to be the most humorous one in the family or the class clown because they enjoy making people laugh; and they are helpful, committed, kind and loving which is a reflection of their sensitivity to others' feelings. Because they are people pleasers, they feel bad when they feel they have let a person down. They do not handle criticism too well but instead take it to heart and may try to fix the criticism by trying harder and doing more so they will not let the person down again. Letting a person down causes them to withdraw from the relationship.

During the counseling session, Sibling #3 was playing peek-a-boo with me in the camera. He kept going upside down, twisting and turning—just enjoying making me smile. As he continued doing funny things in the camera, I encouraged Sibling #3 by informing him of the positive attributes of his personality—that he is kind, does not like conflict but instead likes to do his best—for example. I asked him how he felt when things do not work out and if it makes him cry. He did not answer. I took that as a "yes." I asked him how he felt about mom and dad reprimanding him for not doing whatever he is supposed to do, and he said guilty. I reassured him that they love him, they must correct him and guide him in the right direction. I asked him if he enjoys making his siblings laugh as well as his classmates (since that is a part of his personality)? He smiled and said yes, a lot. I let him know that is a good thing and to not get in trouble for it. My next question was how he feels when things do not turn out right or the way he expects. He answered that he feels "guilty" when that happens. I questioned his answer—thinking that maybe he does not know what the word means, and he has his own definition. I told him guilty means that he was at fault for something.

Sibling #3 shared different topics of conversation. He expressed that he would like to be a Policeman.

He was concerned about a project that he did for his teacher—that it does not crumble or falls apart before his teacher sees it.

Sibling #1 was the last client to be counseled during this

ninth session. Her dad said the personality test for her was "fairly accurate." The color for Sibling #1's personality is green. A child with a "Green Personality" is fair, respectful, purpose-driven, a thinker, inquisitive, tries to make sense of things and tries to see herself in them.

I explained the definition of personality to Sibling #1. She understood already what personality is. However, I expressed to her that although it is a description of how a person acts—that is, how she behaves; as Christians, we want to be sure to behave as follows of Christ.

Sibling #1 has a huge role to play as the eldest sister and the firstborn child. She must be the first example for her siblings. She is a natural leader, a high achiever, organized, on-time, responsible, and obeys the rules. However, there are some negative personality traits for "Green Personality" which must be fostered and guided in the right direction. A few negative traits are as follows: they rarely admit defeat, hate to be wrong; can be bossy; overly competitive; has a fear of failure; a perfectionist—to name a few. Because these negative traits exist, Sibling #1 will need to be guided in a direction that will cause those negative traits to be a positive strength. For example, if Sibling #1 fails at something, it is important to let her know immediately that she is not a failure just because she failed at something.

During her counseling session, we also discussed how her visit was at her mother's home. She said her visit with her mother was good. She continues to journal her feelings which helps to take negative situations off her mind.

SESSION 10

Sibling #4 was first for the counseling session. It was about ten o'clock in the morning. She began making funny faces in the camera. She said she misses her classmates but does not want to go back to school. She said she does not like anything about school.

Sibling #4 celebrated her birthday. She began to tell me what she received for her birthday. She said she received: clothes, earrings, mints, pajamas, mints, a chocolate birthday cake and wigs, ice-cream, and glitter for her "LOL Surprise" dolls. She said she did not have that much fun because she did not go anywhere. She felt like if she had gone somewhere, she would have been happy. (She continued making funny faces in the camera as she spoke to me.)

Since she had a problem not getting along with her big brother, Sammy, I asked her how things were with the two of them. Her answer is repetitively "good." I asked her what she feels like doing today, she said she wants to go everywhere. (This is because she is tired of being in the house because of the pandemic.)

Sibling #3 was next to be counseled. As usual, I greeted Sibling #3 with a cheerful hello how are you doing? He said he was doing good and that he never has a bad day. I asked him about school, and he said it was good. He shared with me that he had a good time at his mother's house although there was nothing to do but play and eat. He said he likes to read about fishing. He was excited to tell me that he has his own fishing rod.

When I asked about him getting along with his siblings, he expressed that they are getting along but it is not that good. I asked him why it has not been so good at home. He said because they have chores and must do work; and that playtime and going outside is boring because they do the same thing every day. He said there was no fussing or name-calling by his siblings. He enjoys playing with Legos, walkie-talkies; and was doing just that while being counseled.

After asking him about having anything to talk about he said yes and that he wets the bed, and he feels embarrassed about it. I asked him if his siblings know this and if so, what do they do. He said they tease him about it.

It was Sammy's turn for counseling. Sammy said he was doing good; and his day was going well. He shared that he was doing well academically in school as well regarding math, science, and reading. He missed being in the classroom.

He said the exciting thing that happened that week was his sister's birthday. Although he was excited about his sister's birthday, there was still arguing fussing, and telling each other what to do. He did express that "she stopped messing with me so much." I asked Sammy what change you made for her to not "messing with her so much?" He said he did not make a change, his dad told them to stop messing with each other. Sammy expressed that he does not like to be close to his sister (Sibling #4). He said he would rather be at least three feet away from her every day. I asked him what happens when she is not three feet away? He said he gets grumpy. I asked what she does to make him feel grumpy. He said she tries to make him laugh and he doesn't like that; and that she's *mean* to him so he tells her to get away from him. My response to Sammy was that she wants his attention. I suggested that maybe doing something that both like and enjoy will not seem annoying to him. (Sammy began texting me during the counseling session.)

I asked Sammy what kind of games he likes to play that Sibling #4 likes to play as well. He said that he only knew of one and that is "hide and seek." I encouraged him to play it with her and she will have your attention that way. (The goal was not for Sibling #4 to have her. It was simply to find a common ground for both to help keep the peace.) (Again, while counseling Sammy, he was typing words— "moment," "Facebook!2" as he put his foot on his face while talking.) He said his sister will follow him if he walks away. I encouraged him to keep a good relationship with Sibling #4; and while he does that, he is teaching her how to keep a good relationship with him and others.

In this Session Ten, Sibling #1 was last to be counseled. She usually presents herself wearing a hoodie and is not that interested in counseling so early in the morning which is understandable. She said she has been doing good and her day was boring so far. She was looking forward to the last day of school for the summer especially because she has been in the house.

Sibling #1 was excited to share with me that she decorated inside her home for Sibling #4's birthday; as well as requested a vanilla and chocolate frosting cake on her sister's behalf.

I inquired about her last visit with her mother at her place of residence. She expressed that it was the same as usual—watched television all day; and her mom barely spent time with her and her siblings during their visit with her. She did not have any concerns and nothing to discuss during the counseling session. She said her quiet time is staying in her room doing nothing; and that she prefers to do nothing during quarantine—there is nothing that interests her but arts and crafts, she exclaimed. She seemed upset and disappointed as she shared that she and her siblings have more restrictions at home than at her mother's place of residence.

Sibling #1's conversation began to change when the focus was turned on Sibling #4. Sibling #1 said began to discuss her behavior and attitude and how it affects her. She said everybody is nice except for Sibling #4. She said her sister is still being mean. I suggested doing something constructive when she feels Sibling #4 is being mean. One of the solitary things I suggested was exercising. Sibling #1 seemed to have made an excuse for everything I suggested, although this is not common. Sibling #1 is about to become a pre-teen who is unhappy with the way things are going in her life as far as her parents are concerned. She is expressing signs of depression. Sibling told me that she does not like exercising because it causes her to lose her breath. (While she was talking to me, she was biting her nails.)

SESSION 11

Session Eleven began with Sibling #4. Sibling #4 has a personality that is very joyful with excitement. She seems to be the social butterfly of her family. Her laughter is contagious because it is like no other.

I encouraged her to be the best "Sibling #4" she can best; never let anyone change who she is; never make fun of anybody; and to make sure she doesn't do any name calling because of how deeply it hurts others.

When I began the session asking about her schoolwork, she did not seem to happy about school. At this current time in school, she was learning how to tell time. The conversation about school changed and we began to discuss how she relates to her siblings.

As the youngest child, Sibling #4 is portrayed as one who is self-centered, competitive, bored easily, likes to be pampered, has a good sense of humor, is outgoing and, finally, enjoys attention.

Sibling #4 began to express that her siblings call her "brat." I inquired why. I asked her what is happening for her siblings to label her with negativity, in other words. She proceeded to tell me that Sammy calls her a brat, he hits her, and he aimed at her with his hanger and a "stretchy thing" in his hands. I suggested to Sibling #4 to speak to them the way she wants them to speak to her; for example, when I asked Sibling #4's siblings through her, while they were in the background, to please be quiet, they did not listen to her. This might have been typical and expected because Sibling #4 is the youngest, however, Sibling #4's voice is somewhat blocked-out by her siblings. It is important to let Sibling #4 know she has a voice, is worthy of being heard and that she is valuable.

Sibling #3 said he did not sleep well, and he woke up early. He said he was looking forward to going to mom's house. He said when he goes to his mom's place of residence, he will be there for three days.

I asked Sibling #3 if he has any concerns or if there is anything he wants to talk about and he said no. I asked him what is he doing to keep busy? He said he prays, have creative time, he enjoys black history and reading. I encouraged him to continue reading. I asked him if he has been getting along with his siblings and he said it has been pretty good. I asked him what's "pretty good?" He said nothing bad. However, he said that Sibling #1 calls Sibling #4 a brat. After questioning Sibling #3 about him calling anyone a name, he said not really, no.

Since there's been much protest for racial justice and protesting against police officers to have them defunded, it was a concern about how the siblings felt about so much going in the world since they've been hearing it discussed on social media and on other electronic devices? Sibling #3 said he was scared, mad, and sad. He said he did not understand much about it. When I asked him what he saw and heard to make him feel the way he feels he said his dad told him and he is mostly scared because of the killings. I explained to him that protesting is not a bad thing; it should be done peacefully. (As I was sharing this information with him, he was making faces in the camera because he was able to see his reflection.)

It was Sammy's turn for his counseling session. He said he was doing good—that he had schoolwork to do virtually because of the pandemic. I asked him if there was anything happening that he wanted to discuss. He said there was nothing serious other than his skin itching a lot because he had an allergic reaction to seafood. He was taking medication for it.

Every week he is scheduled, along with his siblings, to spend time with his mother at her place of residence. He said he was looking forward to going there to eat and play games.

His relationship with Sibling #4 has not changed much. Although wise counsel has been given to both Sammy and Sibling #4, they choose to argue. Interacting negatively with each other gives them attention from their father. However, it is not quite the attention they want from their dad. Their dad intervenes and both get reprimanded.

I asked Sammy what happens when he and Sibling #4 argues while they are with their mother and he said she tells them to sit down. (While counseling Sammy, he turned the camera sideways and began to make faces.) He said the arguing continues for a long time.

Sammy changed the subject and told me what was concerning more at the time. He told me that someone in the neighborhood became extremely sick.

I asked Sammy that with so much going on in the world on the outside of where he lives, how should it be on the inside of where he lives? He answered with a question, "good?" I encouraged him to treat his siblings (and them as well) the way he wants to be treated. I suggested that he remind Sibling #4 to be a good girl. He sadly said that he does not think she would do that.

As an assignment, I encouraged Sammy to right in his journal, read his devotionals (since he and his family do that together each morning. He replied that he does writing in his journal, his daily devotionals, prays, and drawers in his journal.

Sibling #1 was last to be counseled for this session. She did not have much to say. However, she was willing to answer questions. She said she was bored. One of her assignments from the last session was for her to write in her journal thoughts and prayers. She could not understand why people reacted to the virus. She said because it is not worse than the flu (influenza).

I encouraged Sibling #1 to enjoy playing outside and she refuses because of mosquitoes. She added that she is glad it is the month of June because she's going to Savannah, Georgia. I asked her what she is going to do there, and she said she is going to visit her grandparents and cousins.

My concern was her and Sibling #4 while out of town in Georgia. She said that Sibling #4 is nice when she is happy and excited. She said she does not talk to her siblings because they do not listen to her. I asked her why they do not listen to her and she said because they are younger that she is. Although there is a three-year difference between her and Sammy, who is Sibling #2—after Sibling #1, Sammy is not as mature as she is. Sibling #1 is almost a teenager.

Sibling #1 says she has no friends and no one to talk to. I asked her about the things she likes to talk about. She did not have an answer. However, I imagine it is about what teenagers enjoy talking about. She said she does not have any friends at church or at school even before the pandemic caused everything to be closed. She said she has one friend who she has access to on a social media platform.

Sibling #1 was showing signs that she was affected by the impact of her father and mother's divorce. Her favorite color used to be pink or purple; and now it is the color black. She used to enjoy dressing like a princess with flowy dresses. However, she now wears hoodies and does not enjoy playing with dolls anymore while she is in the 5th grade. She is now beginning to like the things that her mom likes—picking up her traits and dressing like a "tom-boy." She said she wants to be like her mom; and wants her head shaved on one side like her mom's head is shaved. I shared with her that it's okay to want to be like her mom but to also remember that she is her own person—that she has her own personality—style, likes and dislikes; and the importance of copying the good that she sees.

SESSION 12

Sibling #3 was first for his counseling session. He seemed to be in a good mood. He shared with me that he interacted with his mother through talking about "this thing called 'childhood.'" I asked him what about childhood did he discuss? He said that his mother always tells he and his siblings to "stay in a child's place." I asked him what he thought that meant and he said, "act like a child." I asked him when she tells him that; and what is he doing when she tells him that and he said she tells him that "at random times." Since that conversation seemed uncomfortable for him, I changed the subject to inquire about his relationship with his siblings since I last met with him for counseling. He said there was less name-calling, and his siblings were not being as mean as usual. He said they had chores and they worked as a team. According to Sibling #3, he did not have anything important to talk about, so I met with Sammy next.

Initially, Sammy did not seem to be in such a good mood. It was because he did not sleep well. He said he stayed up for a long time before going to bed; and eventually had to awake early.

His visit at his mother's place of residence was the same—ate breakfast, lunch, snack, dinner, watched TV and played games on his electronic device. Sammy said he had an opportunity to sit and speak with his mother. He does not enjoy being there too much with his siblings because he said there was a "bunch of arguing and being mean." He said they have not been getting along—especially with him and Sibling #4, who has the same personality as Sammy. Sammy exclaimed that Sibling #4 hits him and he gets mad about it. Since Sammy is the second oldest and Sibling #4 is the youngest and a girl, he is not allowed to hit her back. I asked Sammy what he does when he feels mad with Sibling #4? He said he argues with her and tell her to leave him alone.

Sammy wants a better relationship with his siblings and especially Sibling #4. However, I let him know that for them to have a better relationship, he must do something different regarding her. Sammy mentioned that he does not get along with his eldest sister as well. He said he does not know why they do not get along. I asked Sammy how he would like his sisters to treat him and he said, "the way you supposed to—good and with respect." He knew this was important. I encouraged Sammy by letting him know that if they treat each other better now, they are setting up a good relationship for later when they are also.

My next question to Sammy caused my eyes to open wide because of his answer. He is heartbroken about how he is treated by Sibling #4. He expressed regarding her that he wishes she were not in his life (in other words) because she's *mean*. He expressed his preference for his existence because of his relationship with Sibling #4. He said he does not like Sibling #4 close to him. I encouraged Sammy to remember the good things about Sibling #4 to help change his mind about her. I told him to think good thoughts about her and to see her the way he wants her to treat him.

The conversation shifted to thinking good thoughts in

general because Sammy was speaking as if life was not as precious to him because he did not understand the importance of managing his emotions and practicing self-control. Therefore, I asked Sammy about the good that happened. He said he played with his toys; but he did not know if he felt good while playing with his toys.

I asked Sammy if he felt the same way that he felt the first time he came to counseling. He said, "yes." At that moment, he did not care about his life because of the bad things that happen. What Sammy meant by "bad" was being bothered by his siblings—name-calling and being mean.

At this point, which was the close of this session for Sammy, he needed to be reminded of the things he has—love, a family, things he likes; as well as affirmed him.

Sibling #4 was ready for her counseling session with smiles. As usual, I asked her how she is doing, how did she sleep and how is the day going for her. She responded with a smile by saying, "good." It's important to ask how her time spent with her mother was; so I asked her about her visitation time and she said it was good because she played on the cell phone and the tablet and it was fun. I asked if she had a chance to speak with mom [intimately]; and if she does "girly" things with mom and her answer to both was no. I asked her if there was anything she wanted to talk about and she answered no. It was a concern of mine about how they got along in between counseling sessions; so I asked Sibling #4 how were things between them and she said (although I didn't ask specifically) she's not being mean and she's leaving them alone. I mentioned to her that Sammy said he is angry with her and if she knows why. She said no, she does not touch him or say mean things to him. Because she was specific, I thought that is exactly why Sammy is angry with her. I asked Sibling #4 if she would prefer to be in a separate place from Sammy and if she loves him. I also asked her if she knows what love is. I continued by saying that when you love someone it is all good things you want for them and to do for them. After I thought she understood, I asked her what she is going to do regarding getting along with Sammy and not making him angry. She said she is going to "stop doing the things he said he doesn't like." This is what I left Sibling #4 with to help her keep this in mind.

Sibling #1 has been consistently going last because she seemed to need time to get herself together emotionally and physically.

We discussed the importance of being her own person—being who God created her to be. I encouraged her to discover things she likes; and I used the example of when she was a few years younger, she liked to dress-up, ballet. It was okay for her to like how someone else's style. However, there is a style in her that she will never find in others. Therefore, it was important for her to not become what she saw because what she saw was not necessarily a style please to God. Sometimes wearing a certain style can portray a lifestyle that is not godly. Sibling #1 seemed to understand what I was expressing to her.

We talked about how she has been since the last time we met for a counseling session and she said that things were boring because she cannot go anywhere. (The pandemic continues to have places shut down.) I asked her if she had anything that she wanted to discuss with me and she asked me if I knew of anything they can do for the summer so she won't get bored. I was glad to share with Sibling #1 the various things she can do such as: play jump rope, write with chalk, play pick-up sticks, play steal the bacon, etc. I also included reading comic books since she enjoys comic books. To end the counseling session, I emphasized to Sibling #1 to make her own desires match God's desires; and that this can be done through reading the Scriptures since she does a daily devotion with her family.

SESSION 13

Sibling #3: Sibling #3 said he had a good morning so far. He is very observant and complimentary because he complimented me on my hair which I thought was sweet of him. He was looking forward to the Fourth of July. Because he likes school, he was not glad school was out. He received an excellent progress report which consisted of all A's for the first time. He said, "I never not got one." I encouraged him to keep up the good work.

Sibling #3 said he had nothing in mind to talk about. I asked him how he enjoyed the weekend since he visits his mother just about every weekend. I asked him what did he and his siblings do besides play and go on the computers? He said he only has one book at his mother's house, and he does not know where it is. He continued telling me that his dad has a lot of new books and he read at least most of them.

Sibling #3 shared with me that his favorite color is purple and that he had a purple cartoon vitamin; his helmet is purple, and his bike is black, red, and white. He wanted to show me his purple picture that he drew that was in the art bin in the bedroom. He was so excited about showing me his green paper mache fish; a four-headed dragon; an everything sandwich; and a picture of his favorite video game. His favorite video game is Lego marvel avengers.

Sibling #1: Sibling #1 was second in her turn to be counseled, surprisingly. She said she was tired because she did not sleep well. She was glad to have a new bean bag cushion which is for watching television and lounging around. She likes to watch "America's Got Talent" while sitting in her new chair.

She received her report card. I asked her how she feels about her progress in school; and her response was that she did not know how she feels anymore. She said she does not feel any way. I asked her what she would like to see? She replied that she wants to see everyone go back to school and do what they normally did. She expressed that she would be happier going back to school. She has mixed feelings about being home.

Sibling #1 did not have much to say. I asked about an update on her journal writing. She writes Scriptures in it but felt like if she does not feel anything you do not write your feelings. She is correct about that.

Sibling#4: After checking to see how Sibling #4 was doing, she shared with me that Sammy hit her with a pencil, and it went into her hand. Therefore, she did not see me after her usual turn after Sibling #3. She had been crying and her dad had to take care of her hand and speak with both children.

Sibling #4 said she went to her mom's house and played games, with toys, no dolls, and she and her siblings went swimming. She did not seem so happy that she played by herself. Instead, she desired to play with Sammy's Legos. She said there was no name-calling among her and her siblings. The conversation took a turn with Sibling #4 talking about "Dora the Explorer."

Sammy: Sammy said his visit with his mother was good. He mentioned that he went to the pool. It was obvious that this was a highlight of their weekend. He was glad to jump in the 4-5 feet level of the swimming pool.

I asked Sammy about what happened regarding Sibling #4's hand. He expressed that he was tapping a book with a pencil and he shoved the pencil into her hand. He continued saying that he does not like her and what she does. I explained the seriousness of what he did and how it can be worse if it was someone else; that he cannot handle situations that way; and before he takes situations into his own hands, he should tell an adult because the consequences could be extreme because what he did is considered an assault. I also reminded Sammy of who he is because although he did something so dangerous and threatening, he still needed to be reminded of his identity; that is, he needed to be affirmed.

SESSION 14

Sibling #3 seemed a little sluggish this morning because he did not sleep well, he said. However, he said he was happier at that moment than he usually was for not having to go to school. He was on vacation from school and spent his vacation at his mother's place of residence. He did the usual activities which was watched TV every day; played games, played on the computer, etc. He said it is hard to focus on the important stuff although he said there was not much that he considered important. He shared with me that he was working on a comic and papers were torn out of his book, which he was upset about. I asked him if he can start over and he said he did not know; so, I asked him if he wanted to start over and he said, no. It was not easy trying to find comforting words, but Sibling #3 was eventually okay.

We discussed several other things such as his family Bible

study, how he has been getting along with his siblings which he felt has improved. Since things seemed to have improved, I questioned Sibling #3 about what he thought made the difference so he can use and apply it each time.

Sibling #3 had a deep secret and concerned that he trusted me with. He shared that Sammy made a threat against everyone. I asked him why and he said he did not know. However, it was over a phone that Sibling #3 was playing with along with a black and white phone that needed to charge. Sibling #3 said he was mad about the whole incident. I let him know that it was not his fault and that no one deserves to be threatened, especially, over a phone and a charger. He said his mother told Sammy to apologize and to go to his room to think about what he said. Sibling #3 said Sammy stayed in the room for a long time, but he does not know how long. I asked Sibling #3 how he felt now, and he expressed how "mad" he is. However, he said he and Sammy have continued to speak and get along.

Sibling #3 and I talked about anger and feeling angry. I let him know that it is okay to be angry and that it is not a sin. However, if he acts upon the anger in a deconstructive way, that is when it becomes a sin. I shared the Scripture which says,

"Be ye angry, and sin not: let not the sun go down upon your wrath:" (*Ephesians 4:26, KJV*)[9]. Anger is an emotion that we feel when someone does another wrong deliberately. It is not a negative thing to feel anger because it is a way to express emotion. Feeling angry also allows a person to find a way to feel better or find a solution for what caused the anger. Sibling #3 seemed to have understood that he was not wrong in the way he felt. Because he does not usually experience being as angry as he was, it was important to encourage him to steer his anger in a way that was constructive.

Sibling #4, as usual, was ready for her counseling session. She shared with me that she exercised during her visit at her mother's place of residence. She had a short time at the pool, played games, watched television, played on the tablet and the computer. She is not ready to go back to school towards the end of the summer; yet she wants to stay home by herself.

One of the concerns that Sibling #4 had was that she felt that her dad did not play with her enough while indoors. She expressed that she loves when her dad turns her upside down

---

[9] King James Version Bible. (2012). Holman King James Version Study Bible. Holman Bible Publishers Nashville, Tennessee

and wrestles with her. After sharing this concern of Sibling #4, he informed me that he interacts with her and she is not lacking in that area (in other words). I can agree with that because of Sibling #4's personality type which says she's an extrovert and sociable—to name a couple. Sibling #4 left the session cheerful.

Sammy smiled when he showed his face on the camera during his virtual counseling session. He shared with me that he did not sleep so well because the light that he is able to see while waiting to sleep disturbed him. The solution that was given to him was to turn his back to the light if possible and/or keep his eyes closed. Sammy needed to also understand that there are other factors that contribute to not sleeping in a timely fashion such as diet (what he ate last), and what is on his mind before bed. Reading a Scripture from the Holy Bible helps to keep positive thoughts before sleeping.

Sammy discussed how much he enjoys his watch which is an iTouch. His watch shows how many times he runs, jumps; and he can record his voice and learn games such as math games. This eventually began the conversation about him threatening his brother (Sibling #3). I asked Sammy what he thought about what he said to him and he said he felt wrong—it was wrong.

We discussed emotions and controlling his emotions; things he can do instead of choosing something destructive when he feels anger. I asked him what he is going to do when he gets angry and he said exercise, do learning games and math. Sammy's watch (iTouch) was one of the tools that was brought to his attention as a tool to use to help keep him from anger.

Sibling #1 tolerated counseling. She preferred to remain alone in her bedroom or watching television or on her tablet. She spent the week at her mother's place of residence. This was vacation for Sibling #1 and her siblings. She feels there is nothing interesting to do there; and she does not get to choose what she wants to watch on television. This is not necessarily a bad thing because Sibling #1 is not a teenager and still needs to be guided and guarded against what she should not see and hear. There are many negative influences accessible to children that should be banned.

Since Sibling #1 enjoyed watching television and being actively involved in fun, I encouraged her to create a schedule of things she would like to do and show it to her mother to see if she can make it happen for Sibling #1 and her siblings. A few games that I suggested to her was silent ball, decorating flip-flops (sandals), playing *UNO*, and swimming.

Sibling #1 has a birthday in a few weeks but is not looking to it. She wants to remain a little girl, skip her lower to mid-teenage years and go right to age 18 so she can move out to live on her own.

For her birthday, Sibling #1 went to eat at a restaurant. She also had a "Daddy-Daughter Date." She had an unforgettable time with her father.

SESSION 15

Sibling #3 was sad during his counseling session because he felt like he was not having a good summer break; and he cannot do anything fun.

We discussed how things have been going at home. Sibling #3 said things were not going so well at his dad's house. However, at his mom's house he said things were not going so well. He had a bad experience that he will probably never do again. He said, "This time yesterday I was taking a bath and sniffed up water and stayed in the bedroom until bedtime." He could not watch TV or play games because he did something in front of the camera of the laptop when someone was on a virtual conference where each person and see one another. Sibling #3 was remorseful. I explained the importance of him not doing that again; as well as the repercussions of doing something like that. He understood and felt very sorrowful about his bad behavior and will more than likely not do it again.

Sibling #4 had an injury and had no problem letting me know about it. She burned her thumb this morning. She was still talkative although she was injured. She expressed the different events at her mother's place of residence. She said she watched TV; played with dolls and beanie boos which are stuffed animals with tags that include a birthdate. She said her brother, Sammy, wanted to name the girl parrot, "Sammy" although her beanie boo was a girl.

Since she mentioned in the previous session that she wanted her dad to play with her more, I questioned her about it and she said he had been playing with her more; and that it's been going well.

Sibling #4 mentioned that her cousin was visiting her, and it made her glad. She expressed that her and Sammy were doing well together and getting along—no hitting, no being mean and no arguing.

Sibling #4 was scheduled to go to the pool today and was looking forward to it. She had in mind that snacks were going to be available during her trip to the pool. She was excited and felt that everything was going good with her siblings. I reminded her to keep up the good work in getting along with her siblings.

Sammy's turn was next for counseling. He shared with me that he used his iTouch because he got mad at Sibling #4. This helped take his mind off feeling annoyed by Sibling #4 and others. He shared that he sat by himself and he enjoys that.

Sammy said he enjoyed being at his mother's house and that there was nothing too bad that happened—that it was just a normal weekend. I questioned him about his visit to his mother's place of residence.

Since Sammy had an opportunity to spend time with his cousin, I asked him how they get along. Sammy expressed that he does not like amber being at his mother's house with him because she does not listen much; she doesn't obey the seat belt law for safety; and she doesn't obey her own rules.

Sammy expressed that there are three things he does not like: 1) the quarantine; 2: the pandemic floating in the air; and 3) online school; and that he cannot see his friends often.

To end this session, I encouraged Sammy to continue writing in his diary and journal which included designated Scriptures.

Sibling #1 was next to be counseled. She said that she was bored. Her countenance showed that she was not interested in being a part of the counseling session. However, this is what her dad instructed because he wants her to have someone who she can speak with whom she can trust and feel free to express her feelings to.

After asking Sibling #1 about how she enjoyed her weekend. She immediately spoke about what was on her heart the most; and that was her cousin. She expressed that Sammy constantly gets angry with their cousin because their cousin is "violent"— that is, she hits people all the time.

Sibling #1 said they only spent the night at their mother's place only one night. She said they did not have many activities to do; they just watched television. Their cousin's mother (Sammy's aunt) is said to be lots of fun because she likes to go to the mall and eat a lot.

We talked about school for the new school year and Sibling #1 said they will have virtual meetings and conferences and meetings at the park.

Sibling #1 was not looking forward to her upcoming birthday because she does not want to grow up. She wants to go back to being a baby. This is understandable because she did not have the hardship of how she is currently living. Because Sibling #1 is the eldest child, she had most of the attention for a long period of time. She did not have to visit two separate homes to see both parents. What she enjoyed about celebrating birthdays was planning and decorating her siblings for their birthday.

SESSION 16

Sibling #3 was ready as usual to meet for his morning counseling session. When asked about he is doing and how he enjoyed his breakfast, his response was not with excitement. He sounded like his usual breakfast is raisin bran which he did enjoy because he smiled after sharing this information. He said he slept well but awoke tired. After watching television, the night before without paying attention to the time, he went to bed two hours later than usual.

Sibling #3 was excited about telling me about his karate lessons the day before. He said he did "jumping jacks." He is looking forward to going to his mother's house to ask her to download a new game on the tablet or on her phone.

Sibling #3 went to his paternal grandmother's house; but said he did not remember what he did there. He said his mother had lots of fun too. This was good to hear since he had a problem in the previous sessions about how he felt about some things at his mother's house.

Since Sibling #3 enjoys drawing, I asked him if he has been drawing recently; and he said with excitement, "why didn't I think of that?" He did not draw but he said he read a couple of books. He mentioned his cousin's behavior has been somewhat good; and Sammy and his cousin has been relating well.

Sibling #4 was eager to tell me things she did over the weekend. A fun activity that she shared was playing with a big Barbie Doll who is very tall. It kept at her mother's house and it belongs to her sister, Sibling #1. She expressed that she also enjoys playing with a smaller doll named Carrington.

After asking about her relationship with Sammy—if they have been getting along better, Sibling #4 it's been fine because "daddy made it nicer. After we got in trouble, Sammy got nicer." However, he still says no when she when she asks him if she could play with him. What she does thereafter is go and play with her toys by herself or her sister would play with her.

Sibling #4 says she has been feeling happy. I asked her what makes her happy and she said she does not know; she has just been happy. I asked her if she is looking forward to attending school which is about to open and she said, no because she is going to a new grade. I encouraged her and by reminding her that going to a new higher grade means that she is getting smart. When I asked her what she wants to be when she grows up, she said she does not know. I asked if she likes animals and if she wants to be a veterinarian and she said, "no, I want to be held all next week and all year long. I don't want to walk." Sibling #4 seems to be missing being a baby and/or her times of cuddling from her parents. She receives love from her parents but the interaction she currently receives is not as physical as it used to be.

Sibling #4 was excited about showing me her dolls. She told me she shared her dolls with her cousin at her grandmother's house. She said her cousin was not listening. She kept playing the same game repeatedly. It seemed her cousin could have used some reminding about practicing good behavior. There have been many complaints about the cousin misbehaving repeatedly.

Sammy enjoyed his stay at his grandmother's house. He said he had fun. However, the fun ended whenever his cousin was around because she did not listen. Sammy expressed to me that he did not like her because of this. Sammy, with frustration, expressed to me that he had to constantly tell his cousin to put on her seatbelt while riding in the car. She did not listen to what was right although she knew that was the right thing to do.

Sammy was not looking forward to school, as it was quickly approaching in a couple of weeks. He was still looking forward to going to inside the school building. However, he was not sure of what he was going to the school building. During the counseling session, Sammy's countenance began to change as if he was upset. Sammy was upset because a rubber band that he was playing with would not work for him. I encouraged him to try again and/or ask for help so he would not get frustrated over a rubber band anymore. It was important for me to let Sammy know to protect his feelings—that is, let him know that a rubber band or any object is not worth his emotional stability, mental health, and well-being.

Sibling #1 discussed her visit at her grandmother's house as well. She mentioned that her cousin had the same behavior—not listening and obeying what's right for her.

The news reported an earthquake this morning on this day

and Sibling #1 felt the earthquake. She said she thought were stomping downstairs where she lived.

I asked Sibling #1 if she did any journal writing. She expressed with excitement about her party planning for Sammy's birthday. She is looking forward to a family reunion and not her birthday (as stated in the previous session); however, there will be party bags at her drive-by birthday celebration.

Sibling #1 enjoyed hands-on activities like most children do. However, her personality was of somewhat of a person who was an introvert, yet a leader.

SESSION 17

This is the last Session with Sammy and his siblings. It was not planned; however, their father thought it was best because they just began a new school year and they had to get used to a new schedule. From this day forth, his dad will continue to reinforce the important principles I helped his children within regard to relating to one another and others. This is vitally important in their time of social interaction with other children and in their future relationships. Some of those principles are treating others the way they would like to be treated; don't call anyone bad (negative) names, but instead give compliments to each other (everyone has good qualities); no fighting but instead tell your parent; be constructive (do things that will help you); if someone doesn't want to play with you or you don't want to play with anyone it's ok, we all feel the same way sometimes; when feeling angry, frustrated and stressed, change your thoughts to something happy and do something fun; don't take things out on the other; it's fun to share, etc.

Sibling #3 was aware of who his new teacher was and was excited to see all his friends virtually. In the first week of class, he said he did not have much to say in class and that he was very distracted. This last session with each child was very short.

Sibling #4 was in school virtually as well. She had cereal before her class and was ready to see her friends and classmates. She talked about her recent visit at her mother's house which was the usual—watched television, played with her toys, and played on the laptop as well. She expressed that she tried to play with her brothers, but they told her she could not play with them. The closest she played with them was standing near their bedroom door and found something to entertain herself. She ended her counseling session talking about her toys.

Sammy came to his virtual counseling session looking sad. It was because his electronic devices were not working correctly. He said school is good. However, there was nothing different about it. He said he sees his classmates online but was not glad about it because not one of them were his friends.

Sammy did not have much to say. He recently went to his mother's place of residence and there was nothing different that he spoke of there. Because of his consistent sad countenance, I asked him if everything is okay and he said no, he is mad because his electronic devices are not working correctly. I encouraged him to focus on the positive things so his whole day will not seem defeated. I suggested that he take moments to think about things that are good, so the moment will not take up his whole day. Reminding Sammy of his upcoming birthday seemed to help him change his thoughts to worse. Sammy retreated in his mind to "I never asked to be born." Although he said this, I reminded him that he has a purpose and that he should finds thoughts in his mind to keep him cheerful; as well as do thinks to keep him busy constructively like play with his iTouch watch.

Sammy was given these affirmations and a prayer to pray against depression and suicide:

AFFIRMATIONS:

I AM THE BOSS OF MY FEELINGS.

MY FEELINGS ARE NOT RIGHT OR WRONG; IT IS JUST MY FEELINGS.

IT WILL NOT BE MY BOSS.

I LOVE MY FAMILY AND THEY LOVE ME.

I AM A GOOD SON AND BROTHER.

I CHOOSE TO LOVE WHEN I AM SAD JUST AS I LOVE WHEN I AM GLAD.

MY MORNING PRAYER:

THANK YOU, GOD, FOR LIFE. THANK YOU, JESUS, FOR LOVING ME.

HELP ME EVERYDAY TO LOVE YOU RIGHT BACK—EVEN WHEN THINGS DON'T GO MY WAY.

HOLY SPIRIT, THANK YOU FOR BEING HERE ON EARTH WITH ME, TO LEAD ME AND COMFORT ME, ESPECIALLY IN TIMES WHEN I FEEL SAD—IN THE NAME OF JESUS, I PRAY. THANK GOD, AMEN.

Sibling #1 was in a meeting in virtual school; therefore, she did not have a counseling session.

Ultimate Goal of the Seventeen Sessions

The most important goal of the counseling sessions which were a total of seventeen sessions was to change Sammy's perspective on what he was currently seeing and believing which can be considered fearful and lonely. Sammy counseling sessions began because he not only contemplated suicide, but he also attempted suicide. However, he did not follow-through with it. Each time we met, I gave Sammy, especially, a compliment, something positive to think about, and left him with encouragement.

Was the goal accomplished? Will Sammy contemplate or attempt suicide again? What homework assignments would you have given Sammy and his siblings if any?

The goal of sharing information about what suicide is, the repercussions of suicide and how it effects family members was accomplished. Getting to the root of the issue that caused Sammy to attempt suicide was accomplished. However, I hope Sammy does not gear his thoughts towards the condition that he is living under which caused him to be deeply depressed arrive again. I hope Sammy does not contemplate and attempt suicide anymore. I gave Sammy tools to change his perspective about life and himself. In addition, I gave his siblings tools to get along better. The answer is the identity—that is, knowing who you are, loving others and yourself and forgiving one another.

Is There An Age of Accountability?

The Bible is filled with Scriptures about children, their role as a child, the role of the parents to help guide their children, the consequences of their actions and the example they are to be as believers. When children are infants—in their months—they begin to learn and understand right and wrong, good, and bad. What we usually define what is good and bad, right, and wrong is called morals. Children are taught morals. They learn quickly to say "no" because of their parent telling them what they can have, what they can touch, what they can eat or taste, etc. They usually learn quickly what is hot [to touch] and what they can touch. They also sometimes learn at a very early age why they should not go in the street. Their understanding begins to grow as they grow older; along with their willingness to learn. There are Scriptures that help us to discover if there is an age of accountability in the Bible when it comes to salvation. I believe it is based on the child's understanding.

Since before my daughter was born, while in the womb, I would read Scriptures aloud to her so she could hear it at the prenatal stage that her hearing was in the process of developing. Upon her birth, in March, I continued to read and pray aloud so she can become more familiar with having a spiritual life. Along with the rest of my family, I would take her to church. I would purposely sit towards the front to get her used to church behavior. I wanted her to learn when to be loud and when to be quiet, which was during the Scripture reading and preaching.

From infancy, I taught her what was right and wrong; and to use good manners along with training her up the way she should go (at her level of understanding). She practiced what I taught her and has not in her toddler age gotten into much trouble.

When my daughter turned four years old, she noticed a witnessing tract on the kitchen table called *"This Was Your Life."* She asked me about the tract, so I explained it to her the way

I thought she would understand. I led her to Christ through explaining the tract and explaining *Romans 10:9.* She was happy that she had become a born-again Christian. *Matthew 19:14 says, "But Jesus said, Suffer little children, and forbid them not, to come unto me: for of such is the kingdom of heaven"*[10].

Today, I continue to lead her to holiness and righteousness through reminding her to keep God first when she awakes. It is automatic for her to read the Scriptures and to complete her daily devotion before play and utilizing her electronic devices. She knows the difference between right and wrong at her level of understanding. *James 4:17 says, "Therefore to him that knoweth to do good, and doeth [it] not, to him it is sin"*[11].

Many people compliment her on her sweet spirit. She is conscientious about honoring me as her mother just as the Scripture says. *Proverbs 20:11 says, "Even a child is known by his doings, whether his work [be] pure, and whether [it be] right."*

Even at the age of ten, she is considered a little child, with a

---

[10] King James Version Bible. (2012). Holman King James Version Study Bible. Holman Bible Publishers Nashville, Tennessee

[11] King James Version Bible. (2012). Holman King James Version Study Bible. Holman Bible Publishers Nashville, Tennessee

pure heart and one who believes quickly with her faith in God. Therefore, I believe if God decided to take her, she would be with Him in heaven. *Deuteronomy 1:39 says, "Moreover your little ones, which ye said should be a prey, and your children, which in that day had no knowledge between good and evil, they shall go in thither, and unto them will I give it, and they shall possess it."*

At the age of twelve, Jesus went to the temple to preach the Word. *Luke 2:42-43 says, "And when he was twelve years old, they went up to Jerusalem after the custom of the feast. And when they had fulfilled the days, as they returned, the child Jesus tarried behind in Jerusalem; and Joseph and his mother knew not of it."* Eventually, Mary and Joseph found Jesus in the temple among doctors and leaders asking questions. He was at the age that he understood. Jesus astounded the doctors and the people who were there in the temple because of his great understanding. Even then, He was still the Son of the God.

Once parents teach children the difference between right and wrong; and the difference between good and bad, they will be held responsible for what they are taught, and God will judge them. *Romans 14:12 says, "So then every one of us shall give account of himself to God."* Therefore, the age of accountability is based on God's will and judgment.

Is Suicide Okay for Children to Commit?

Suicide is never okay for anyone. Only God knows if a child understands in their heart what suicide is. They may have an idea of what they believe it to be. However, if children are at an age where they understand *"Thou Shalt Not Kill" (Exodus 20:13)* they understand to a certain extend that taking your own life is wrong, although they may not know the repercussions of taking their own life.

Suicide, according to Dr. Nelson Newman in his book, "Defending the Faith Through Counseling," he says that "suicide is, 'the act of designedly destroying one's own life.' The fact that it is one's own life that they are taking does not negate the fact that suicide is still murder which God commands against. (*Exodus 20:13*) God has a plan and will for each person's life which includes a timeline. When one commits suicide, they are stepping outside of that will and putting an end to God's plan before its due time. (*Ecclesiastes 7:17*) God alone is the one who is to give and take life (*1Samuel 2:6*) but the one who commits suicide is playing the part of God."

Dr. Nelson goes on to say that, "sadly enough, the average person knows of someone who has committed suicide. The Bible too, records the suicide of several men." There are at least three reasons why people commit suicide: 1) because of shame and guilt as did Samson (Judges 16:30) and Judas Iscariot (*Matthew 27:5*); 2) because of the fear of consequences bring others to their limit as did Saul's armor bearer. (*1Samuel 13:5*) Still others, like Zimri (*1Kings 16:18*), committed suicide because of general despair over a situation. The common element among them all is depression. Depression is almost always evident in the life of the suicidal. They have allowed the circumstances of life, and often their distorted view of the circumstances, drive them over the edge. What they fail to realize, however, is that suicide is a permanent solution to an often-temporary problem. It is a cowardly and selfish response to one's problems"[12] (Newman, 2016)[13].

---

[12] King James Version Bible. (2012). Holman King James Version Study Bible. Holman Bible Publishers Nashville, Tennessee

[13] Newman, N. (2016). Defending the Faith Through Counseling. Arise & Declare Ministries, Inc.

What is Depression?

Depression is anger turned inward.

I. **Mental illness comes from:**

    a) Chemical, emotional, a traumatic event.

    b) Studies show that when we think repeatedly, it takes a toll on our mental well-being. Some of us have thought ourselves into depression but NOT everyone. When we overthink, we can worry ourselves into a hole. Overthinking and worrying are linked to anxiety and depression.

    c) What is meant by OVERTHINKING? Overthinking is thinking too much or too long.

    d) We can control our thoughts and how we control our thought-life.

II. Do you know what depression involves?

a) Depression is more than sadness. It involves loss of interest, tiredness, sleeping too much, and difficulty concentrating.

III. How do you know if you have experienced depression or if you are depressed?

a) If you have difficulty concentrating; trouble sleeping; low energy to get through the day; loss of interest in spending time with others—usually close family members; tiredness; loss of interest in the things you enjoy; guilt feelings from things that you used to love; not as motivated; closing yourself off from your loved ones.)

IV. What are the symptoms of depression?

a) Little interest or pleasure in doing things.

b) Feeling down or hopeless.

c) Trouble falling or staying asleep or sleeping too much.

d) Feeling tired and having little energy.

e) Poor appetite, overeating or considerable weight changes.

f) Feeling bad about yourself—that you are a failure or having a lot of guilt.

g) Difficulty concentrating on things or making decisions.

h) Moving or speaking slowly, so that other people have noticed or being so restless that you have been moving around a lot.

i) Thoughts that you would be better off dead or of hurting yourself in some way.

What's in a Name?

Calling people by their name, speaking positive to and about people, and most of all knowing who you are is very important in how you view others, what you stand for or represent, and what you allow from people in regards to respect. So, what is in a name? Here are a few Scriptures:

1. *Proverbs 12:18 There is that speaketh like the piercings of a sword: but the tongue of the wise is health.*

2. *Ecclesiastes 10:12-14 The words of a wise man's mouth are gracious; but the lips of a fool will swallow up himself. The beginning of the words of his mouth is foolishness: and the end of his talk is mischievous madness. A fool also is full of words: a man cannot tell what shall be; and what shall be after him, who can tell him?*

3. *Matthew 5:22 But I say unto you, That whosoever is angry with his brother without a cause shall be in danger of the judgment: and whosoever shall say to his brother, Ra'-ca, shall be in danger of the council: but whosoever shall say, Thou fool, shall be in danger of hell fire.*

4. *Colossians 3:7-8 In the which ye also walked some time, when ye lived in them. But now ye also put off all these; anger, wrath, malice, blasphemy, filthy communication out of your mouth.*

5. *Ephesians 4:29-30 Let no corrupt communication proceed out of your mouth, but that which is good to the use of edifying, that it may minister grace unto the hearers. And grieve not the holy Spirit of God, whereby ye are sealed unto the day of redemption.*

6. *Ephesians 4:31 Let all bitterness, and wrath, and anger, and clamour, and evil speaking, be put away from you, with all malice:*

Did Jesus do any name calling?

Jesus knew no sin. He revealed who people truly were. This is coming from righteous anger not human unrighteous anger.

7. *Ephesians 4:26 Be angry, and sin not: let not the sun go down upon your wrath:*

8. *James 1:20 For the wrath of man worketh not the righteousness of God.*

Examples:

9. *Matthew 6:5 And when thou prayest, thou shalt not be as the hypocrites are: for they love to pray standing in the synagogues and in the corners of the streets, that they may have glory of men. Verily I say unto you, They have their reward.*

10. *Matthew 12:34 O generation of vipers, how can ye, being evil, speak good things? For out of the abundance of the heart the mouth speaketh.*

11. *John 8:43-44 Why do ye not understand my speech? Even because ye cannot hear my word. Ye are of your father the devil, and the lust of your father ye will do. He was a murderer from the beginning, and abode not in the truth, because there is no truth in him. When he speaketh a lie, he speaketh of his own: for he is a liar, and the father of it.*

12. *Matthew 7:6 Give not which is holy unto the dogs, neither cast ye your pearls before swine, lest they trample them under their feet, and turn again and rend you.*

Reminders:

13. Colossians 4:6 *Let your speech be always with grace, seasoned with salt, that ye may know how ye ought to answer every man.*

14. Proverbs 19:11 *The discretion of a man deferreth his anger; and it is his glory to pass over a transgression.*

15. Luke 6:31 *And as ye would that men should do to you, do ye also to them likewise.*

Know Who You Are

It is crucial for Christians especially—young and old—to know your identity. That is your weapon against the lies that the enemy tells you. God has given you an identity through the Scriptures and through parents (guardians and caregivers). *Training up a child the way they should go (Proverbs 22:6)* is included in teaching them their identity; affirming children daily is giving them their identity to know who they are and whose they are[14]. This is a weapon against the negative labels and name-calling. It is important to tell and remind children that through Christ:

---

[14] King James Version Bible. (2012). Holman King James Version Study Bible. Holman Bible Publishers Nashville, Tennessee

- *I am a good person*

- *I am intelligent*

- *I can put negativity behind me*

- *I am loved*

- *I can rejoice in my abilities*

- *I have many talents*

- *I have confidence*

- *I am not a victim*

- *I can look forward to each new day*

- *I no longer feel the need to control others*

- *I can affirm my worth*

- *I am a loving person*

- *I am a friendly person*

- *I can forgive continually*

- *I can praise regularly*

- *I am a capable person*

- *I am not alone*

- *I am emotionally calm*

- *I respect myself*

- *I can respect others*

- *I feel happy*

- *I am at peace with myself and others* (Affirmations by Dr. Marlin Lance).

Intervention Recommendations for Child Abuse and Childhood Trauma

Children who are experiencing trauma and maltreatment are suffering in silence. Many parents are taking their struggles out on them through rejection, abandonment, physical abuse, sexual abuse, etc. This population is important because, as you can see in the world today, children are least threatening, vulnerable and are easily influenced; that is, they trust adults quickly. Children are being used and abused—used as pawns with parents who are separated and/or divorce; and sexually violated by their mother's boyfriend, sibling, father, stepfather, grandfather, or a close family member. The size of the population of children who experience trauma is not accurate. However, just to give an idea of the amount, the size of the population of the children who experience trauma and maltreatment is approximately 4.3 million according to the American Society for the Positive Care of Children[15]. This population needs help with getting these numbers down tremendously so children can live a peaceable life. What must be taken into consideration is that children who are victims of maltreatment struggle with sleeping at night, they struggle academically, socially, and emotionally—to name a few. Some parents are oblivious to this while other parents do not seek help for their child and/or their self. Parents need help in training and raising their children. However, the pride, guilt and shame could be the stumbling block for help in intervening and preventing child trauma and maltreatment. There are types of intervention and preventative measures against child maltreatment while this heinous crime continues. However, governmental programs and State agencies have the tools to assist families who are in this predicament with children who are suffering in silence.

---

[15] https://americanspcc.org/child-abuse-statistics/

Interventions

- Available interventions for child maltreatment are information that social services have compiled for child maltreatment, any legal contributions that's appropriate to integrate, law enforcement, and professionals in the hospital industry, mental health facilities, as well as educated professionals who have vital information.

- Community leaders and neighborhood-based efforts of the community can contribute by encouraging residents and supporting their efforts to enhance and upgrade the programs and self-help programs for children and families. Children who have experienced maltreatment are not commonly in an environment where there is local effort and support for them and their families.

- Administering child-centered efforts on behalf of the child's safety and personal integrity allow for the intervention to take place on behalf of the child's best interest.

- Focusing on the support of family needs strengthens the family to function better and enhances their ability to manage. This will assist in preventing child trauma and maltreatment.

- What I have found that is available for children who have and still is experiencing trauma and maltreatment is medical examinations. This will help to detect internal injuries such as broken bones and bruises; an STD test to discover if the child was sexually abused and contracted a sexually transmitted disease. Another means of intervention is psychosocial testing to observe the children's behavior to detect abuse. What is available to help child trauma and maltreatment is child protective services. They are trained to detect any kind of abuse in children through valid testing.

Treatment

Treatment for children who are experiencing trauma and maltreatment is counseling, building their confidence, encouraging them, and letting them know they are loved and have a purpose. Reassuring children who are victims of trauma and maltreatment should be reassured that it is not their fault. Assessments, evaluations, and observations will allow child trauma and maltreatment to surface from the child and their behavior to be detected for a means of intervention, analysis, and to provide statistics from the evidence collected. This may not be an immediate means of intervention because time is a factor in a child who experienced trauma and maltreatment. They need to feel comfortable enough to speak to the social worker or the person performing the evaluations.

Recommendations

In addition to recommending having the child evaluated through counseling sessions, observations at the child's home, monitoring, it is important to develop a plan for the family to receive counseling as well. Educating parents about child abuse prevention and other types of preventions promotes change and healing in the home.

Parent training may be more effective when the child does not have other mental health difficulties, when the conduct problems are less severe, when the family has fewer socioeconomic disadvantages, when the parents are together, and when parental conflict and stress are low. Parent training may also have larger effects if the parents have high levels of social support and the parents do not have a history of antisocial behavior or psychiatric difficulties themselves. More research is needed to confirm all these suggestions (Fonagy, Cottrell, Phillips, Bevington, Glaser, & Allison. 2015)[16].

The ideas I have about how I would know the intervention is working is through observations after counseling sessions. I would see if the tools that I have given the child has been used. That is how I know if the intervention is working. The change I would want to see in the client is changed behavior along with a genuine smile. Behavior opposite from what I initially observed during the psychosocial evaluation. This may sound simple; however, child trauma and maltreatment are not a "smiling matter" for a child. The average child is usually observed to be a smiling, joyful and friendly child. However, a major issue such as child maltreatment can snatch the attributes of a child away from them.

There are factors that can influence preventative measures against child trauma and maltreatment:

- The parent and child and their interactions (microsystem).
- The familial and community contexts within which the parent-child dyad is embedded (exosystem).

---

[16] https://www.nationalchildrensalliance.org/media-room/national-statistics-on-child-abuse/

- Societal contexts comprising overarching cultural and social structural elements within which the parent, child, family, and community settings are themselves lodged (macrosystem).

These spheres of influence are not static. Bronfenbrenner includes the chronosystem to account for changes in these various domains over time. Throughout the life of a child, the relative influence of these spheres may change (Faugno & Speck, 2017)[17].

In conclusion, we cannot completely stop child trauma and maltreatment—the beatings, the neglect, the sexual abuse, and murder by their parents and caregivers. We frequently hear of these horrible stories of the lives of innocent children who severely suffer by the hands of their parents. The discovery of the child sometimes seems like an episode of the television show, "Law and Order" when children are either found starving, tied up somewhere, drowned in a bathtub or a pool, or discovered some other gruesome kind of way. Child welfare and Child Protective

---

[17] Alexander, R., Faugno, D. K., & Speck, P. M. (2017). Child Abuse Quick Reference 3e : For Health Care, Social Service, and Law Enforcement Professionals: Vol. Third edition. STM Learning.

Services continue to be overwhelmed with child trauma and maltreatment cases. However, there are tools to advocate and intervene on behalf of children who are experiencing trauma and maltreatment that are put in place to protect them and their families against further harm and danger. Programs for intervention and prevention for parents is important to put in perspective the social, political, economic, and religious challenges of the past (Scannapieco & Connell-Carrick, 2005)[18].

---

[18] Maria Scannapieco, & Kelli Connell-Carrick. (2005). Understanding Child Maltreatment: An Ecological and Developmental Perspective. Oxford University Press.

References

Alexander, R., Faugno, D. K., & Speck, P. M. (2017). Child Abuse Quick Reference 3e : For Health Care, Social Service, and Law Enforcement Professionals: Vol. Third edition. STM Learning.

https://www.nationalchildrensalliance.org/media-room/national-statistics-on-child-abuse/

https://americanspcc.org/child abuse statistics/

https://www.nap.edu/read/2117/chapter/9

King James Version Bible. (2012). Holman King James Version Study Bible. Holman Bible Publishers Nashville, Tennessee

Maria Scannapieco, & Kelli Connell-Carrick. (2005). Understanding Child Maltreatment: An Ecological and Developmental Perspective. Oxford University Press.

Newman, N. (2016). Defending the Faith Through Counseling. Arise & Declare Ministries, Inc.

Peter Fonagy, David Cottrell, Jeannette Phillips, Dickon Bevington, Danya Glaser, & Elizabeth Allison. (2015). What Works for Whom?, Second Edition : A Critical Review of Treatments for Children and Adolescents: Vol. Second edition. The Guilford Press.

Printed in the United States
by Baker & Taylor Publisher Services